Prentice Hall Regents ESL

Taking Care of the EARTH

PRENTICE HALL REGENTS
A VIACOM COMPANY

LITERATURE PART 1 FICTION

Getting Ready to Read

Look at the "Before" pictures. Look at the "After" pictures. What happened? How could people help?

ecology	garbage	factory	wildlife	ocean
environment	dump	chemicals	farm	land
pollution	truck	smoke	forest	air
polluted	highway	fumes	meadow	breathe
dirty				clean

Are the following statements *true* or *false*?

1. People do many things that harm the earth.
2. There is nothing we can do to help protect animals and the environment.
3. All forms of life and the environment are connected to each other.

twine	**oil tanker**
wound	**dolphins**
unwound	**tusk**
Arctic Ocean	**recycling**
iceberg	**mustangs**

LITERATURE
PART 1
FICTION

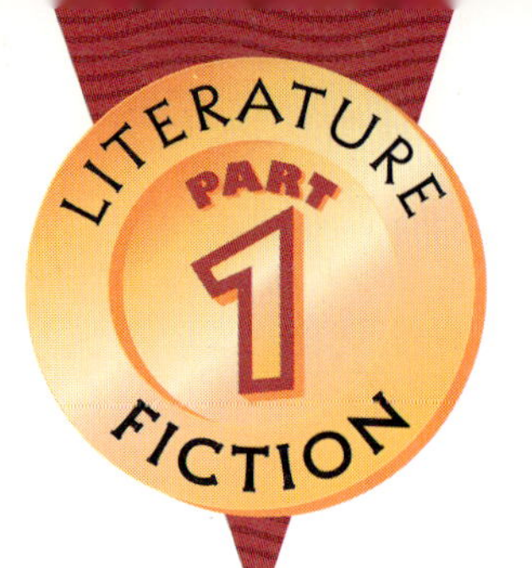

The Earth Game

By Pam Conrad

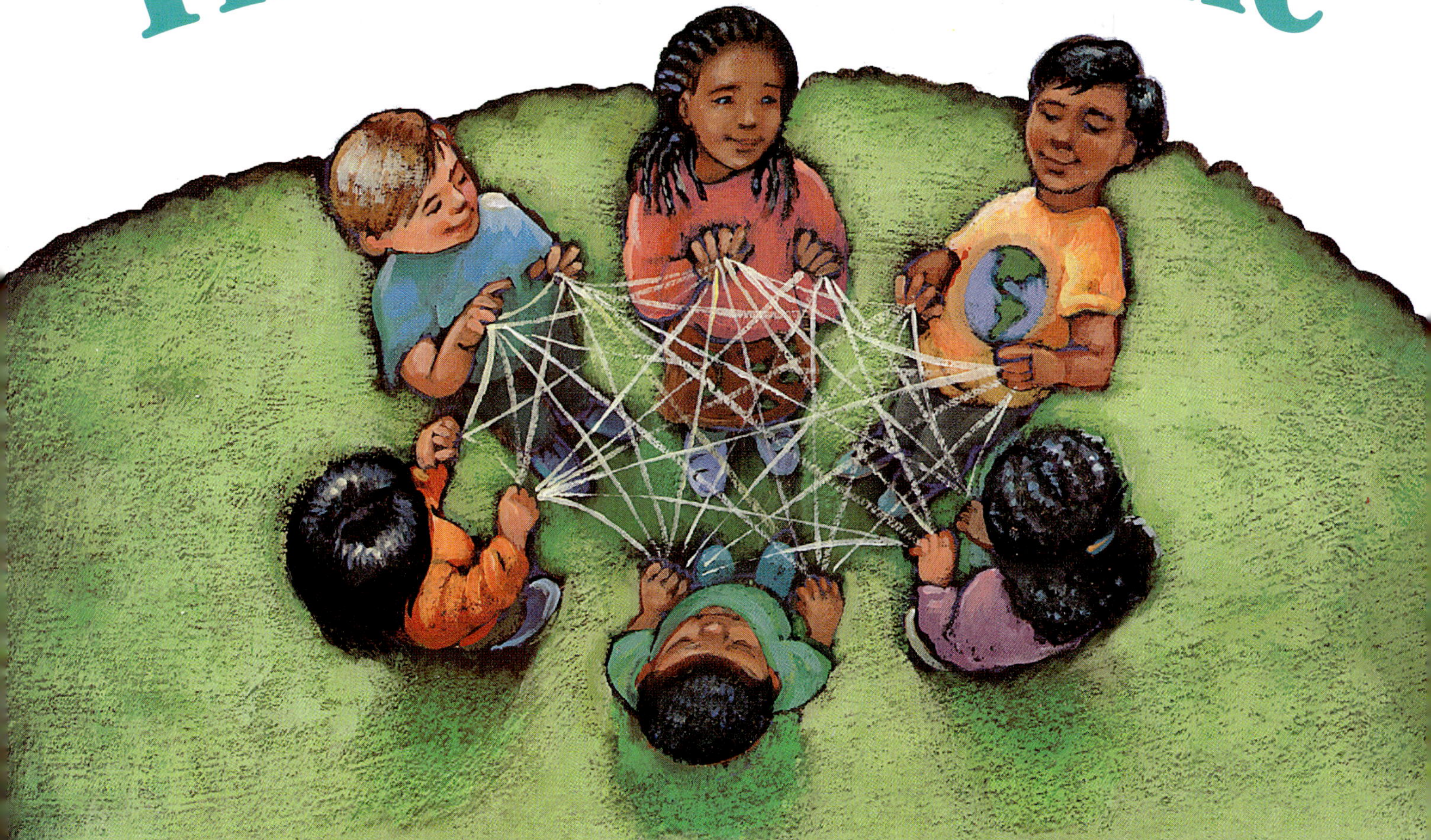

Not very long ago, in a meadow not too far from here, some children found a ball of twine lying in the grass.

"Watch me," called the oldest girl. And she tied the end of the string to her finger and tossed the ball in the air.

Her brother caught it and wrapped the string around his own finger. Then he pitched it across to his friend.

The twine unwound just enough as it sailed through the air. His friend caught the ball, wrapped the string around his thumb, and threw it over to someone else.

After many tosses back and forth, the ball had unwound to just a loose end, and the smallest child wound that around his finger. And there they were, joined in a circle by the twine that wove a net at their center.

"Now look," said the oldest girl, and she wiggled her finger.

"I felt that!" said her brother.

"So did I," said his friend.

And standing very still, one by one, they each wiggled a finger until they could feel the twine move with even the gentlest tug.

"Now, let's be the Earth," said the girl. She closed her eyes, and her voice lifted over the meadow. "I am a jungle in Africa, and someone is shooting an elephant for his tusks." She moved her finger. They all felt the tug and grew sad.

"I'm the Arctic Ocean," said her brother, "and an oil tanker is hitting an iceberg and spilling oil over me. Soon all the birds will be black and slick and won't fly anymore." He tugged, and they were silent.

"I am a big city, and no one can see the stars in the sky because the air is thick with smoke and fumes from my factories." The gentle tug passed around them.

"I was once a farm, but the sunflowers and rows of corn are gone. Today I am a mall." They each felt the sad tug.

They stopped tugging. It was as though a thick cloud had passed before the sun and darkened their day. It was very still, except for a bird whizzing by over their heads.

Then the smallest boy smiled. He moved his finger. "I'm a town, and in a backyard somebody's putting out seed for the winter birds." He tugged again, and their faces lit up.

"Yes!" The tallest girl raised her hands, and the pull was felt by all. "I'm a highway, and people are walking alongside me, picking up bottles and cans for recycling." She wiggled her fingers and laughed, and they could all feel it.

“I’m a neighborhood, and people are planting trees along my concrete sidewalks.”

“I am an ocean, and fishermen are freeing the dolphins from their nets.”

“I’m a herd of wild mustangs, and someone has given me land and turned me loose.”

“I’m a lonely country road, and somebody’s painting my mailbox red.”

They all laughed. Then they raised their hands, lifting the net of twine higher and higher. They could feel the certain pull of all the things people could do to make a better world.

After You Read

Say these sentences. Match each one to a picture above.

1. The air in the forest is clean.
2. Smoke and fumes pollute the air.
3. People are cleaning up the highway.
4. This garbage dump was a forest.

Decide whether each thing is "good for the earth" or "bad for the earth."

1. People ride bicycles instead of driving to work.
2. People kill animals to make coats.
3. School cafeterias use plastic dishes once and throw them away.
4. People turn off lights when they leave a room.
5. Farmers feed garbage to pigs.

Getting Ready to Read

grizzly bear

red wolf

American crocodile

three-toed sloth

golden parakeet

great green macaw

howler monkey

The animals on the map are endangered. These species are in danger of disappearing from the earth. Once they are gone, they will be extinct.

woodlands	**plains**
rain forest	**ocean**
mountains	**continent**
species	**endangered**
habitat	**extinct**

1. Where does each animal live? Describe its habitat.
2. What is happening to all of these animals?
3. Why do animals become extinct?
4. Do you know any other endangered species?

Gone Forever?

Black Rhinoceros

A snow leopard roars in the high mountains of Asia. A black rhinoceros thumps across the plains of Africa. A grizzly bear scoops up a fish in a North American river. A mother blue whale and her calf glide through the deep waters of the ocean.

All these animals share the earth with us. They thrill us with their beauty. We love the way they move. We love the way they look and the noises that they make. But just loving them is not enough! All of these animals are endangered. Many of them have died, and without special care, they may someday disappear from the earth.

Why is it important to care for animals like these? One reason is to protect the balance of life on earth. Another reason is the beauty of the animals themselves. Each species of animal is special. Once it is gone, it is gone forever.

by Barbara Reeves

African Elephants

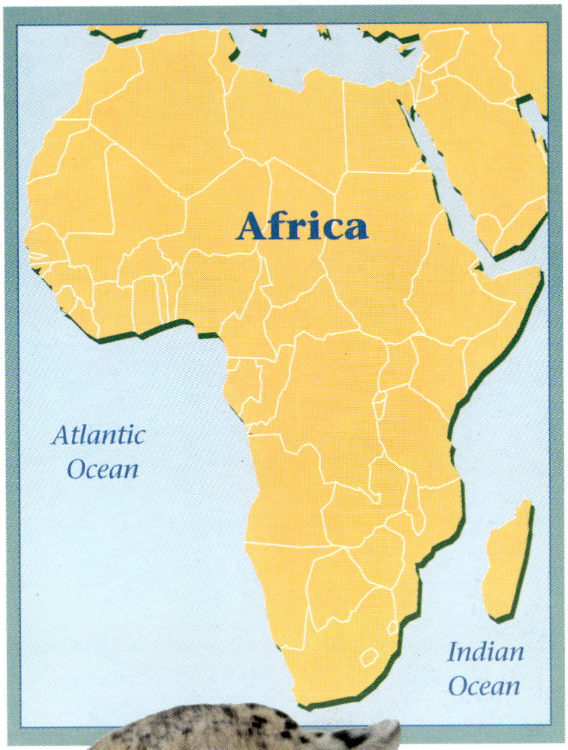

Africa

Atlantic Ocean

Indian Ocean

Africa was once filled with wild animals. But things are changing fast.

The black rhinoceros lives on the plains of Africa. It has very poor eyesight—and a very bad temper! Even though the black rhino can be dangerous, it can't escape hunters. Hunters kill rhinos for their horns. (This is because some people think the horns have magical powers.) This has helped place the black rhino on the endangered list.

The elephant seems to represent all that is strong and wild in Africa. It once had no natural enemies. It is now endangered—killed for its ivory tusks.

The world's fastest land animal, the cheetah, also lives in Africa. It, too, is becoming extinct as people take over the land and crowd out the cheetah.

Imagine Africa without the rhino, the elephant, or the speedy cheetah. Once they are gone, they are gone forever.

Cheetahs

Three-toed Sloth

North America
Atlantic Ocean
Pacific Ocean
South America

Wherever people are careless about the land, there are endangered species. Grizzly bears like to wander. Each bear needs up to 1,500 square miles of homeland. Today, because forests have been cleared to make more room for people, the grizzly's habitat is shrinking and the grizzly is disappearing. It joins other endangered North American animals, such as the red wolf and the American crocodile.

In South America, destruction of the rain forest threatens many animals. Unusual mammals, such as the howler monkey and the three-toed sloth, are endangered. Beautiful birds like the great green macaw and the golden parakeet are also becoming extinct. They're losing their homes in the rain forest, and thousands die when they are caught and shipped away to be sold as exotic pets.

Great Green Macaw

Grizzly Bear

The giant panda of Asia is a fascinating animal. Yet there are only about 1,000 left in the wild. The giant panda eats mostly bamboo. When bamboo forests die, so does the panda. China is trying to protect these special animals.

Asia's big cats are also in trouble. The snow leopard lives high in the mountains. Even there, it faces loss of land and hunters who kill it for its fur. The tiger, the largest of all big cats, is hunted for sport.

Snow Leopard

What about the oceans? Animals are in danger there, too. The blue whale is the largest animal in the world. It weighs up to 390,000 pounds! Whale hunting and pollution are this species' enemies.

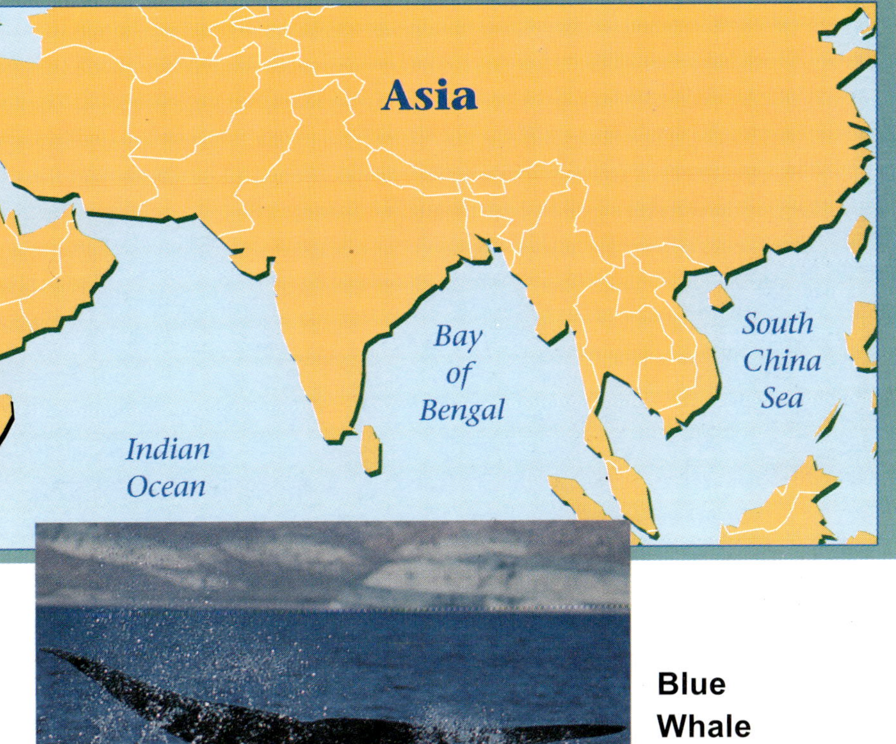

Blue Whale

People cause most of the problems that animals face. We change or pollute lands. We hunt animals for skins, fur, tusks, or horns. We destroy animals that get in the way of farming or building. And we bring them home as pets.

What can *you* do to help endangered animals? Learn as much as you can! The more you know, the more you can help.

Support zoos and wildlife groups. Many zoos breed endangered animals. Contribute to groups, such as the National Wildlife Federation and the Sierra Club, that work hard to protect animals. You can also be a wise shopper! Never buy a pet that has been raised in the wilderness.

The world is made up of many living parts. Each part depends on all the others. If even one species becomes extinct, our world changes. When we talk about beautiful wild animals, let's hope that we never again have to say, "Gone Forever!"

National Wildlife Federation
1400 Sixteenth Street, N.W.
Washington, D.C. 20036

Sierra Club
730 Polk Street
San Francisco, CA
94109

After You Read

Name each endangered animal. Match each animal to the main reason it is endangered. Discuss your answers with a partner.

1. Hunters kill them for sport.
2. Hunters kill them for horns, fur, and tusks.
3. People buy them as pets.
4. Their food source is disappearing.
5. The ocean is getting polluted.
6. People are cutting down forests.

The animals you see below are already extinct. In pairs or groups, talk about each animal. Tell where you think it lived, what it ate, how it protected itself, and why it is now extinct.

dodo

apatosaurus

saber–toothed tiger

INTO THE RAIN FOREST

RAIN FOREST FACTS

- Rain forests cover about 6% of the earth's surface.
- The rain forest in the Amazon River Basin contains more species of plants than all of Europe.
- The narrow, pointed leaves of some rain forest plants help them shed excess water quickly.

The Amazon Basin

The Amazon Basin contains the world's largest rain forest. It covers 2.3 million square miles in nine different countries. The Amazon River is the second longest in the world and contains more than one-fifth of the world's fresh water.

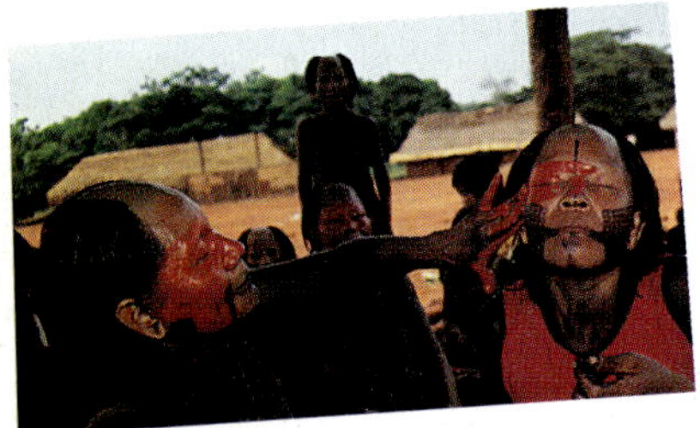

For thousands of years most people of the rain forest did not know anything about the outside world. Now the forest is disappearing and the people have to learn new ways of living. The members of the Kayapó tribe, of central Brazil, have become farmers. They have learned how to grow crops without damaging the soil.

The Southern Bearded Saki or monkey tail duster lives in the rain forests of northeastern Brazil. More than half of the rain forest in its homeland has been cut down. This monkey is hunted for its meat and its tail, which is sold to tourists. It is now an endangered species.

A Rain Forest Snack

Tropical fruits like bananas and coconuts grow in rain forests. Cinnamon is made from the bark of a rain forest tree. You can use these foods to make this delicious snack.

MORE RAIN FOREST FACTS

- A single rain forest tree can support more than 400 insect species.
- Amazonian Indians use the fruit and stem of the Burutí palm as a drink, as the main ingredient in bread, and as a building material.
- An area of rain forest the size of a football field is burned down every minute. At this rate, the rain forests may be gone by the year 2030.

What is Happening to the Environment ?

Save the Dolphins
Save the Whales
Save the Seals

Munch Crunch

1 cup sweetened dried banana chips
2 Tablespoons shredded coconut
1 teaspoon cinnamon

Instructions:

1. In a bowl, mix together all ingredients.
2. Eat and enjoy!

WARNING
LITTERING
Dumping Rubbish Trash or Garbage is Prohibited
Penalty
PENNSYLVANIA GAME COMMISSION

Conserve Water

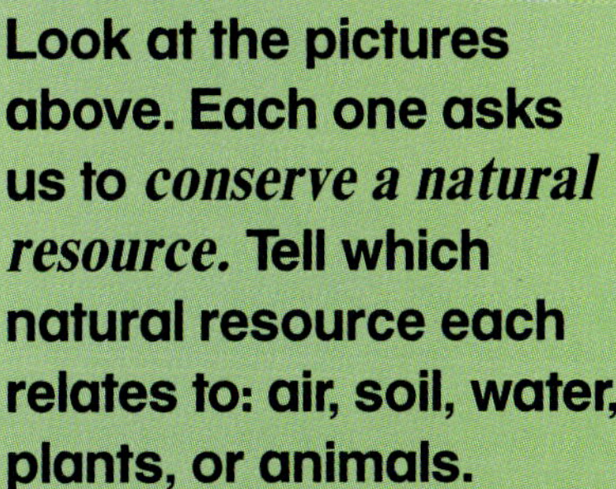

Look at the pictures above. Each one asks us to *conserve a natural resource.* Tell which natural resource each relates to: air, soil, water, plants, or animals.

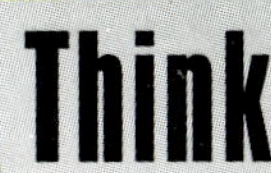

Think about it !

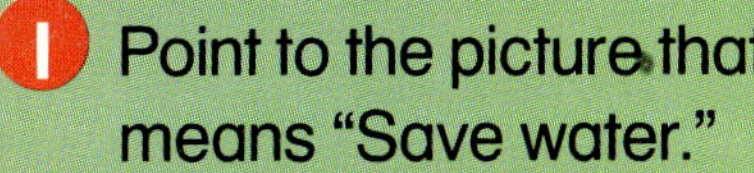

1. Point to the picture that means "Save water."
2. How can you help clean up the environment?
3. What is a car pool?
4. Is eating fish and meat different from killing an animal for its fur?

EVERYDAY TALK

- Asking someone's opinion
- Expressing an opinion

Read the cartoon. Then tell your own opinion about recycling.

An airplane sprays chemicals on crops

Ask a partner's opinion about one of the topics below. Then give your opinion.

- Using lab animals to test medicines and cosmetics
- Wearing fur coats
- Giving money to a "save the animal" campaign
- Using chemicals to grow food crops

You may want to use these expressions.

What do you think about...?	In my opinion...	I think it's a lousy idea!
What's your opinion of...?	What I think is that...	I really don't think so.
How do you feel about...?	If you ask me...	That would be great!

Growing Food

Some rain forest people in Brazil are farmers. They use burned wood as fertilizer and plant banana trees to attract wasps. The wasps kill leafcutter ants that could harm their crops.

1. What advantages are there to using wasps to kill harmful insects?
2. What advantages do chemical pesticides have?
3. Where do the Amazonian farmers get their fertilizer?
4. Where do American farmers get their fertilizer?

In the United States, most farmers use chemical fertilizers to grow large crops. They use chemical pesticides to get rid of harmful insects.

Theme Project

Are you ready to start your volunteer project? Discuss the following. Then decide if you're ready to start.

1

What kind of project will you do?

2

How will you start?

3

What can each volunteer do to help?

4

What can you do to make sure your plan will work?

5

How many classes in your school will join the project? Could you interest more people? Should you make posters to advertise the project?

Theme Games

It's Your World!

(A game for 2–4 players)

Players start on "Home." Each player spins or throws a die and moves the number of boxes shown.

When a player lands on a box, the player describes the drawing and tells how it relates to an environmental problem.

Players continue to take turns and circle the board until "Time" is called.

Scoring: One point for each answer and one point for passing "Home." The player with the most points wins.

Prentice Hall Regents
Publisher: Marilyn Lindgren
Project Editors: Carol Callahan, Kathleen Ossip
Assistant Editor: Susan Frankle
Director of Production: Aliza Greenblatt
Manufacturing Buyer: Dave Dickey
Production Coordinator: Ken Liao
Marketing Manager: Richard Seltzer

McClanahan & Company, Inc.
Editorial, Design, Production and Packaging
Project Director: Susan Cornell Poskanzer
Creative Director: Lisa Olsson
Design Director: Toby Carson
Director of Production: Karen Pekarne

Prentice Hall, Inc.
A Viacom Company
Upper Saddle River, NJ 07458

PRENTICE HALL REGENTS
A VIACOM COMPANY

Printed in the United States of America

10 9 8 7 6 5 4 3 2 1

ISBN 0-13-349788-7

Prentice-Hall International (UK) Limited, London
Prentice-Hall of Australia Pty. Limited, Sydney
Prentice-Hall Canada Inc., Toronto
Prentice-Hall Hispanoamerican, SA., Mexico
Prentice-Hall of India Private Limited, New Delhi
Prentice-Hall of Japan, Inc., Tokyo
Simon & Schuster Asia Pte. Ltd., Singapore
Editora Prentice-Hall do Brasil, Ltda., Rio de Janeiro

Acknowledgments
Grateful acknowledgment is made to the following publishers, authors, and agents for their permission to reprint copyrighted material. The following literature appears in both Teacher's and Student Books:

Maria Carvainis Agency: "The Earth Game" copyright © 1993 by Pam Conrad. Originally published in *The Big Book for Our Planet.* by Ann Durrell, Jean Craighead George, and Katherine Paterson, (Eds.) by Dutton Children's Books 1993. Used by permission of Maria Carvainis Agency, Inc. All rights reserved.

Cover
Karen Blessen

Photography
Doug Cheeseman/Peter Arnold p12; Michael P. Gadomoski/Photo Researchers p27 (top right); John Giustina/The Wildlife Collection p26 (bottom right); Ken Karp Photography p22; Thomas Kitchin/Tom Stack & Assoc. p14 (bottom right); Will & Demi McIntyre/Photo Researchers p27 (bottom); Jack Montgomery/Bruce Coleman p16; C. Allan Morgan/Peter Arnold p14 (top left), p15 (bottom right); Saule Petean/DDB Stock Photo p26 (top left); Kevin Schafer/Peter Arnold p15 (top right); Anup & Manoj Shah/Animals, Animals p13 (all); Norm Thomas/Photo Researchers p20; Martin Wendler/Okapia/Photo Researchers p14 (center right); David Young-Wolff/Photoedit p27 (top left)

Illustration
Daniel Del Valle p18; Jennifer Hewittson p21, p23; Paul Meinel p18–19; Karen Minot p10–11, p17; Stacey Schuett p4–8; Matt Straub p2–3, p9; Ron Zalme p20; Rose Zgodinski p13–16